# RIVER FRIEND

## A series of Riverine Small Books

### by Sylvia M. Haslam and Tina Bone

## BOOK 5

## REED—ON THE EDGE

Fifth Book to be published:

REED—ON THE EDGE

A Book in a series of Riverine
publications by

Sylvia M. Haslam and Tina Bone

(Each book is about a different subject so the
series can be read in any order)

*Written by Sylvia Haslam and
Edited and Illustrated by Tina Bone,
unless otherwise stated.*



RFS5: PAPERBACK **48** pp.
ISBN No. 978 1 9162096 4 0
**60** Illustrations

Published by: Tina Bone UK
First edition: October 2020
Revision (errata): November 2020

**www.riverfriend.tinasfineart.uk**
**Email: ourbooks@tinasfineart.uk**

# CONTENTS

# INTRODUCTION TO THE SERIES

Rivers are vital. They bring freshwater to the land, on which all its life depends. They are beautiful and fascinating, making up both the typical British countryside and many of its most spectacular views. If they vanished, what hardship and outrage there would be! Yet, slowly, slowly, they are vanishing, the larger stream becomes smaller, the tiny brook becomes a ditch and dries, and is filled in—the small ditches get polluted and dug out, become dull, and vanish from sight and consciousness. How can we save our rivers and riverscapes? How can we raise awareness on this slow, almost invisible loss?

We believe that this series of handy, small books, suitable for readers from teenage upwards, will help to raise awareness. Individually, each book tells a story on a particular riverine and riparian environment. Collectively, the series will inform, in a simple and effective manner, the extraordinary value of freshwater and its plants.

The Authors realised that there was a huge gap in the literature. There are many publications for scientists, for pond-dippers, birders and anglers, but "easy-read" books focussing on the river itself, and the vegetation belonging to it and creating the habitat for all else: we could find none!

For explanations regarding British freshwater plants, terminology mentioned throughout the series, and Picture Guide and reference section for further reading, see the book entitled *A PROLOGUE TO THE SERIES: Plant identification and Glossary of Terms* (also available to view in pdf format free on-line at http://riverfriend.tinasfineart.uk/resources/

Other titles in the Series are listed on the last page of this book and on the River Friend Website:
**http://www.riverfriend.tinasfineart.uk**

# REED—ON THE EDGE

## Introduction

*Reed—On the Edge* differs from the other books in the River Friend Series because it describes a single species: Reed (scientifically termed "*Phragmites australis* (Cav.) Trin. ex Steudel, formerly *Phragmites communis* Trin."), which in this book, is just "reed" or "*Phragmites*". Reed grows on the edges of brackish water channels, intermittently on the edge of large, slow, often estuarine and muddy waters, as well as dominating some huge (or small) reedbeds nearby, wet, or at least part-flooded, but not necessarily next to open waters. The word "brackish" first appeared in the English Language during the 1500s, at which time it purely meant "salty," as did its Dutch ancestor "brak". The word still refers to a mixture of saltwater and freshwater.

This book describes the reed plant and how it grows, and also explores why it grows like it does. Much is known—but much is unknown. A great amount of information can be found by watching the life-cycle of just one plant (in this case the reed) as it grows and changes.

In the language of Botanists, the reed can be described as a rhizomatous grass, growing as a collection of upright stems. There may also be surface stems called "*legehalme*" (pronounced "leggerharmer"). Reed has a creeping rootstock system (rhizome) which not only stores food for the growing plant but also enables new growth of shoots and roots. Each stand of growing reed, whether large or small, probably originated from one individual plant which has cloned itself—all plants in that group being genetically identical. Other reed "types" include genetic differences such as resistance to drought, salinity and low temperatures. Colour variations in flower heads range from creamy-white to dark purple.

## Boring?

Well, it is easy to see how anyone finds Reed (*Phragmites*) boring. Reed is just green. No pretty flowers, no stripes or blotches, just spikes with leaves on, one after another, rather like our commonest agricultural plant—wheat—just one shoot after another across a field, and a reed is not just singled out to be jumped upon with joy by plant hunters as something rare and strange. It occurs in reedbeds, which in small, variable England are not all that large, but which reach acres and acres in, say, Iraq, with perhaps 120,000 hectares pre-drainage*, or the Danube Delta where the Volga delta was estimated at *c.* 110,000 hectares (one hectare equals 2.47 acres).

*Boring*—perhaps to many people? To others, a mysterious vision of green waviness, reeds moving in the wind.

In winter, when summer-grazed grass is long and straggly and of a dull, browny green, the damp soil looks black and cold, and dead reeds are scattered round watery edges. Straggly, tussocky grass shows winter has come, its presence showing botanically that there is grazing. In some areas, livestock graze and keep down reed until the ground is too wet, both for livestock and for grass. Even then the reedbed imposes its own fascination, its eerie other-worldness, the sense of moving to a different time and place. A sense greater than the sense of cold and wet is gathered up into the reedbed.

The reedbed is human-size in height and this is part of its uniqueness. A wood dominates a person, a person dominates a heath. But a reedbed may be tall enough to overtop a person by half a metre, so is different to either wood or heath. Above is the sky alone and, in Norfolk particularly, the skies are marvellous. Working all day, surrounded by the reeds, no sound but that of reeds and birds (Fig. 1), no view beyond a few metres except looking up to the blue sky and perhaps remarkable white clouds: an experience not to be forgotten.

Willow-reed (*Salix-Phragmites*) bands enclose undrained lowland streams which have the reeds outside the willows. The willows get the scour from the stream, which they, but not dominant reed, can tolerate. The reed therefore grows out further away from the stream, so having less water, so being shorter: like the reed on railway banks. In wet woodland, whether this is a narrow band of sallow or willow, or a genuine large wood, *Phragmites* is also shorter,

---

* The traditional home of the tribal "Marsh Arabs" (Ma'dān) was in the Tigris-Euphrates marshlands of south and east Iraq until recently when, in 1991, the wetlands were drained during the country's Civil War and the people were displaced. After the war some effort was made to restore reedbed and people—but such is extremely difficult.

Fig. 1. Apart from its invaluable resource for humans, many animals and birds live and breed in the reedbed. For example, Reed Warblers and Bearded Tits (or Bearded Reedlings). Bearded Reedlings eat mainly reed seeds in winter and soft-bodied insects which gather at water's edge during the summer. Their nests are built with reed leaves and old fluffy seed heads. The figure shows a male bird with black moustache, a more plain female, and eggs in a nest in the swaying reed stems.

flaccid and plainly not healthy (Fig. 2). But if "unhealthy" means doing poorly and heading for extinction, that is certainly not so.

*Phragmites* stays, whatever its appearance, for however long the wood stays. There is never a 100% canopy in such woods. The wide-ranging reed rhizomes can produce many shoots in sunlit glades, where the reeds are also taller, shaded for only part of the day; whilst in more shade, shoots are sparser and are rare in the heaviest shade. Light interacts with the structure of the willow (*Salix*) wood and with the behaviour of *Phragmites*. Reeds stay, even with this particular damage-factor.

Fig 2. *Phragmites* in wood, England. Short, narrow, non-flowering reeds, with leaves adjusted to horizontal to catch the most light.

The influence of another widespread damage-factor—grazing—is different. In the wood *Phragmites* stays because light is always adequate, taking the wood as a whole. This is not the case with grazing, which also can be mild but can be more severe and, at its heaviest, eliminates the plant completely. Grazed shoots must be replaced if minerals (food) are in short supply, so grazing kills reed quicker in nutrient-poor habitats. But death comes whether quick or slow, which is not the case in a shaded, wet woodland.

4

Reed populations in Malta are disappearing. How is a nation's *Phragmites* lost? Long-continued drying and disturbance does it very slowly, over decades, and even over centuries. How fascinating, though, is the great range of *Phragmites'* behaviour in the small area left! Dwarf and prickly *legehalme* (stems growing flat on the ground), 3m-tall reed, field reed, reed growing through tarmac, varied genotypes, Crystal-ball Egyptian introduction, and the grass-like remnants at the edge of stone walls at the "rivers" edge, likely to be washed off in the next decade.

What are the uses of reeds and reedbeds? Whole human populations can live in and, in extreme cases, nearly entirely upon the reedbed. The extreme variety of uses from pens to spears, medicine and baskets is most surprising for a plant seldom very obvious to courts, governments and cities, whose citizens prefer to be on dry land.

Uses continue for thatch in England (Fig. 3) and those countries now supplying England's shortage of reed. For a relatively minor, though especially widespread plant, *Phragmites* has a quite exceptional number of uses. Interestingly and unusually, as the old uses fade out they are replaced by new technology, for which, as the others in earlier times, *Phragmites* is the best available plant. Thatching in Britain is, if anything, increasing and thatching reed is now imported here from all over the world, including Europe and China. Some reedbeds in the supplying European countries are conserved because profits can be made from this *revived*, not *new*, use for continental reed. Whilst thatch is considered to be an interesting feature in Britain, it appears that continentals consider it to be a sign of squalor, to be got rid of in the twentieth century.

Fig. 3a. A typical English cottage with a Reed roof. Each Thatcher has their own signature trademark model pattern, animal or bird, also made from reed in a wire cage which they sometimes include in the thatching job—usually perched on the roof-ridge.

Left to right: Thatcher's Cat motif; Thatcher's Bird motif (wire cage under-model, reed rotted out); and, for interest, a beautiful clock, set in lead, on a thatched rooftop.

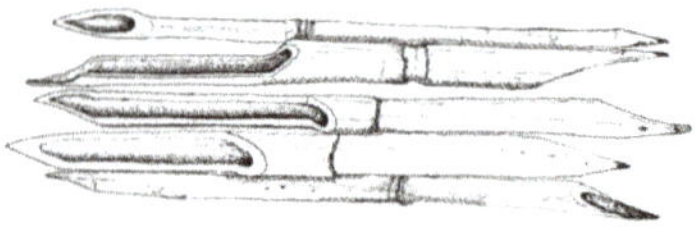

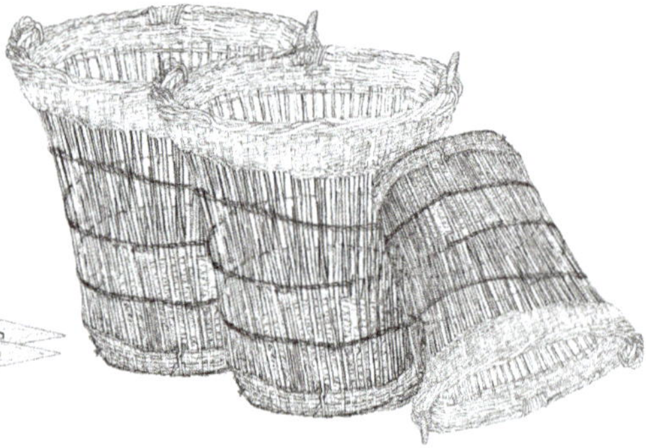

Fig. 3b. Pens, baskets and arrows of yesteryear made from reed.

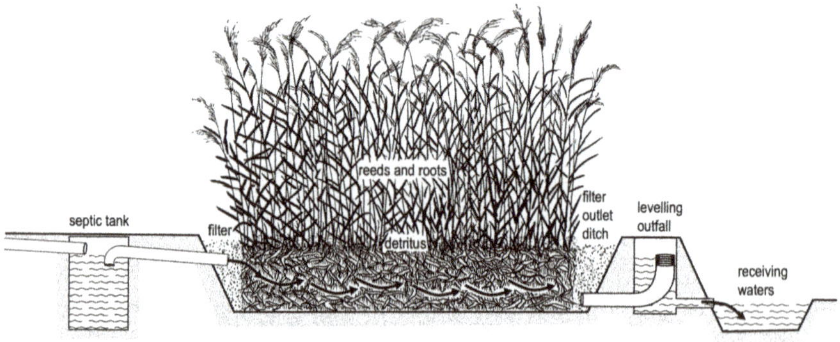

Fig. 3c. One of many designs of a reedbed purification system: reeds are used to treat waste. "Dirty" liquids move very slowly within the dense root system allowing micro-organisms, fuelled by oxygen passing through the leaves and stems, to clean up.

Purification in constructed reedbeds, and in reedbeds planted for this particular reason, is increasing at a great rate. This is a use not really considered in the past. Historically, how far did communities putting waste in the nearest marsh realise it improved dirty water, and how far was it just a convenient dump?

6

Fig. 3d. Thatching reed stacks for roofs, imported to Britain from China and Austria. *(Photograph, courtesy of Peter Brugge, Master Thatchers (North) Limited (www.thatching.net).*

Fig. 3e. On the River Waveney in Norfolk, reeds cut in January from reed beds which grow beside the river are laid out to dry.

Fig. 3f. Another use for reed: a swan has built her nest from reeds, amongst the reeds at Wicken Fen, April 2011.

Fig. 3g (above). *Scirpus lacustris* or Bulrush.

Fig. 3h (left). One way to harvest rushes from the river bed in East Anglia—usually in June, July and August each year—is by hand using a special scythe-type blade attached to a 6ft long handle. Stems of up to 10ft are cut from long punts floating down the river. Stems are tied in bundles (bolts) and stood against a hedge to allow sun and wind to dry them.

*Phragmites* should not be confused with tall rushes such as *Scirpus* [*Schoenoplectus*] *lacustris* (Fig. 3g), which grows in shallow water along the edges of waterways and which, like the reed, has recently regained favour for economic use, Fig. 3h. The revival in the use of cut rushes includes floor matting, basketry, tableware, furniture, hand bags, hats, purses and shoes, as well as learning workshops.

The recent use of constructed wetlands for water purification is still expanding, and in Europe this normally uses *Phragmites*. And how many people gazing at a reedswamp think, "*There is my water storage*"? And probably even fewer think, "*There is my carbon storage, taking carbon from the air, we must not let it be destroyed because of all the carbon that would be let into the air*". The Fenland in Britain, and similar agricultural areas of The Netherlands and elsewhere, attest to this. Every year peat oxidises and vanishes, by perhaps a metre in 25–100 years. This is a huge amount when spread over hectares. What about peat burned as fuel for power stations? For crofts, peat fuel is a small, sustainable loss, but power stations use huge amounts. So do gardeners for horticulture, and new peat is bought each year to counter oxidation. (If every flower bed needed peat just the once, it would still be bad, but not quite so evil!)

Reed is important in so many ways, and since its recorded uses started early in Ancient Egypt, it must be supposed it has been so since *Homo sapiens*—if not Neanderthal man—first invaded Europe, and in Africa before that. Though early man in Africa would probably not have had so many uses for it as there are better plants there for things like spears, pipes and thatch.

The earliest English description of a reedbed is that in Felix's *Life of St Guthlac* (Colgrave, 1956), in AD 730. Guthlac, born around 674, lived in the Isle of Crowland in Lincolnshire between 701 and 715. This was the wet Anglo-Saxon period when Roman drainage had fallen into disrepair. Guthlac's fens had dense reedswamp, isolated reeds, thickets, presumably on small islets, where houses also could be built, and open water with pools large enough to have waves recorded. Guthlac travelled by boat, but feared foes coming on foot. He was tormented by demons (Fig. 4). He lived a life of penance, wore simple animal skins, ate only barley bread and drank the marshy water.

These days much the same habitat can be found in, say, large parts of the Hungarian Lake Tisza (Fig. 5). However, there is a great psychological difference. Hermits, and to some extent monks and nuns, went into the wetlands so that their prayers would purify and sanctify the haunt of demons. Hallucinations and fevers, now ascribed to, for example, malaria, were then considered satanic.

"*Boring*?" Obviously not to everyone!

Fig. 4. A couple of roundels re-drawn, taken from *Guthlac's Roll* (early thirteenth century) which depicts his life in 18 pictures in ink on a vellum roll. *Resource Courtesy of the British Library.*

Fig. 4a. Guthlac being swamped by evil demons.

Fig. 4b. Guthlac appears to King Æthelbald in a dream.

Fig. 5a. The Visitor Ecocentre in Poroszlo contains much information about the rich flora and fauna of Lake Tisza and its surrounding valley.

Fig. 5b. A view of Lake Tisza, Hungary, showing a large expanse of reeds.

## Belligerent?

*"Belligerent"*—that large green grass, just sitting in wet places. A grass, war-like? What a silly idea. But yes, it is in the silent battlefield of the reedbed. We are so used to seeing our gardens where we can put in and take out plants small and tall at our pleasure, and fields where the farmers do the same, that it does not occur that there is a different world of vegetation—when left alone.

A plant is not "nice" to its neighbour—seeing the plant next door has space to grow in, enough light to grow well, enough nutrients and, of course, enough water. When you put new plants in your garden you do all this for the *Geranium* or whatever. What about the weeds that are "in the way" of your new plants? They are the plants that would grow if you allowed them to.

How does a reedbed maintain itself? Reed must be able to grow, and other species must not be able to kill it. Therefore the need for *Belligerence*! In lakes there are few potential competitors. Reed size, together with the space taken up, makes invasion unusual. Where it can shade other plants, it can probably kill. With intermittent drying, reeds are dense enough to cast heavy shade. Becoming a little drier again, there is probably a thick litter mat, again hindering invasion. Only gaps in the reedbed can be colonised.

The basis of *Phragmites'* performance is the emerging bud. If these are many and wide, reeds will be dense and tall. If they are few and narrow, they will be sparse and short. *Phragmites* competes mainly by its thick canopy shading out all below. This means many large buds. There is a minor control over bud-width at ground level, as some species produce a root toxin which can narrow, and so shorten, the emerging shoots. Likewise, litter mats may be toxic. Even the litter mat of *Phragmites* itself, when thick, may be a hindrance to its own growth. These are local (very thick *Phragmites* litter is usually patchy). The ordinary *Phragmites* litter mat helps protect the bed from invasion, and does not poison it.

Major growth control is through the horizontal rhizomes. They store organic food from the aerial shoot above and minerals from the soil and water around. Both food and minerals can be in short supply, and future growth performance may be affected. A few short reeds cannot supply enough food to power a monodominant emergence of reed a few months later. In order to produce many large buds, therefore, the horizontal rhizome must first have enough food to enable it to accomplish this. Secondly, it must receive signals from the rest of the plant about the surrounding environment. Thirdly, plant vigour may vary. An advancing reed margin will steamroller its way through most vegetation. Unless the hinterland has the vigour to maintain dominant *Phragmites*, the advancing margin has little effect on its neighbours. Most stable stands are without advancing vigour, but unless the rhizomes are able to send up a potential canopy, there will not be a dominant stand. Where minerals (or food) are low, such vigour is often also low. It depends, though, on the competitors whether it is *too* low!

Spring-burning (if not scorching the soil) increases reed vigour and buds. This alone may alter the balance in favour of the reed. Conversely, unusual flooding or drought weakens reed and lays the bed open to invasion from other species. The reed used to be burnt off in spring, being just a small part of commercial reedbed management. This was normally done in modest rotational strips so as to preserve several types of habitat and the creatures which lived there at any one time: burning is now discouraged (Figs 6a–c).

An individual study of the effects of burning-cutting was published in 1992 which concluded that:

> "From this short term study, ...management by cutting or burning does not have a major influence on the invertebrate community; total number of invertebrates, species-richness, species diversity and evenness showed no relationship with treatment. ...general conclusion is that careful burning of reed beds is no worse than cutting, but that burning at the wrong time of year, or burning of dry reed beds are likely to cause damage." (Ditlhogo et. al).

Fig. 6a. Traditional burning (Norfolk).

Fig. 6b, left. Manual cutting and gathering of reed (Norfolk Wildlife Trust). Fig. 6c above. Machine cutting for commercial use (River Tey, Scotland).

The anonymous and epic Anglo Saxon Poem, *Beowulf* (*c*. 975 AD), the hero of which battles with a monster named Grendel, a Water Witch, and a fierce dragon, describes a wetland. Now, such reedswamps are full of light, both actually and figuratively (Fig. 7). The actual light has obviously always been there. The eyes perceiving doom and gloom are now fewer.

Fig. 7. A "light" part of the reedbed, Wicken Fen, April 2011. A Grasshopper Warbler is singing in the foreground—becoming a rare sight in Britain, now on the ICUN Red List of endangered species—they do like visiting Britain's fenland to breed in summer, arriving early April each year from their over-wintering grounds in West Africa around Senegal and west Gambia.

After the Anglo-Saxons came the drier mediaeval climate. In 1250 Matthew Paris could write in the *St Alban's Chronicles* that the Fenland was recently transformed from a haunt of black devils to fertile meadows and fields—probably due more to climate, though there was also drainage (Fig. 8a). And, in more recent times (*c.* 2004), the Reed inspired a new pedestrian bridge design (Fig. 8b).

Fig. 8a. "The Monarch of the Fen" stands proud amongst old reed in winter, in front of newly furrowed peat-fields. (*Lifesize water colour painting inspired by this scene seen through a car window, whilst travelling along the A10 near Ely, Cambridgeshire, in 2011.*)

Fig. 8b. Artistic impression of a "Bridge of Reeds", intended to evoke a reedbed.

Reedbeds attract a great deal of talk from national and international organisations but sadly receive hardly any funding for research or conservation. However, most vegetation types receive both, as in ancient oak woods, and some neither, for example, river plants. There is plenty on the value of wetlands, but where is the money even to fence out livestock, let alone stop the abstraction of the underground water which keeps wetland wet? Dry a reedbed and in due course, a woodland is there instead.

Wetlands now tend to involve higher aspirations such as philosophy, beauty, learning, spiritual and humanitarian concerns. Losing a wetland means losing its associated plant species, its flora and its varied, prolific and interesting fauna. It would probably take centuries to replicate the fauna in a new reedbed, with different soil and treatment (Fig. 9). Too many people think it is possible to "restore" a reedbed in new surroundings. To create (or restore) a reedbed, is possible. The vigour and versatility of reed means it can grow in most wet places. To restore the birds is more difficult. Some of them will come whenever they see a habitat. Not all, though, and certainly not all the invertebrates which are needed to make up a true wetland ecology. Broadland has much richness and biodiversity, and there are substantial differences between the various marshes and the Broads. Those are very difficult to restore, particularly when many of the "inhabitants" are still to be found in particular marshes only, and no one knows the reasons for the different biodiversity: was it the mowing of 500 years ago? That, by itself, is a silly question, but the integrated management over the past 700–800 years could well be the cause, and one not possible to emulate (without extremely accurate details of today's habitat; and even then there is the question of dispersal.)

Fig. 9a. The much spoken-about Bittern will normally return to a wetland if conditions are right. Here pictured amongst a managed reedbed at Lakenheath Nature Reserve in 2007 (the male bird is larger than the female, but most other features, including plumage, are the same).

Fig. 9b. This schematic diagram illustrates the enormous diversity of species, both flora and fauna, which are usually found in a Reed Wetland and/or man-aged reedbed. As well as those mentioned here, there are many more species of flora and fauna, including insects such as dragonflies, moths and beetles.

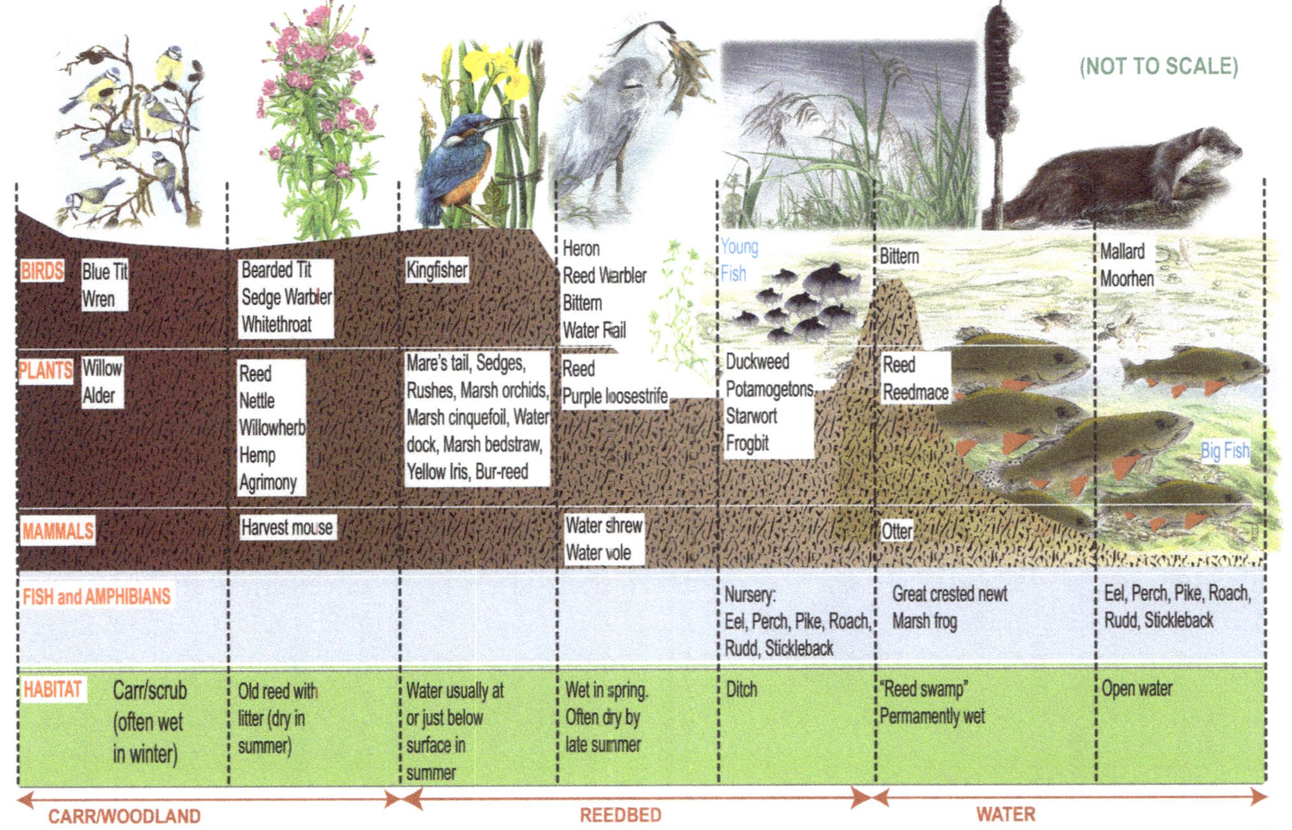


| | CARR/WOODLAND | | REEDBED | | | WATER | |
|---|---|---|---|---|---|---|---|
| BIRDS | Blue Tit, Wren | Bearded Tit, Sedge Warbler, Whitethroat | Kingfisher | Heron, Reed Warbler, Bittern, Water Rail | | Bittern | Mallard, Moorhen |
| PLANTS | Willow, Alder | Reed, Nettle, Willowherb, Hemp, Agrimony | Mare's tail, Sedges, Rushes, Marsh orchids, Marsh cinquefoil, Water dock, Marsh bedstraw, Yellow Iris, Bur-reed | Reed, Purple loosestrife | Duckweed, Potamogetons, Starwort, Frogbit | Reed, Reedmace | |
| MAMMALS | | Harvest mouse | | Water shrew, Water vole | | Otter | |
| FISH and AMPHIBIANS | | | | | Nursery: Eel, Perch, Pike, Roach, Rudd, Stickleback | Great crested newt, Marsh frog | Eel, Perch, Pike, Roach, Rudd, Stickleback |
| HABITAT | Carr/scrub (often wet in winter) | Old reed with litter (dry in summer) | Water usually at or just below surface in summer | Wet in spring. Often dry by late summer | Ditch | "Reed swamp" Permanently wet | Open water |

15

Brilliant?

What are reeds like? To begin with *Phragmites* is one of the very few plants to be native (not introduced) in all five continents of the world. There is least in Australasia: but there it is, sitting in Australia (and New Guinea) (Fig. 10). Next, a reedbed can live a very long time (Fig. 11). Elsewhere peat could form most or all of the core for 8,000 years or more, when the Ice Age was retreating. Peat-forming plants are few, and *Phragmites* is the commonest of those accumulating under water.

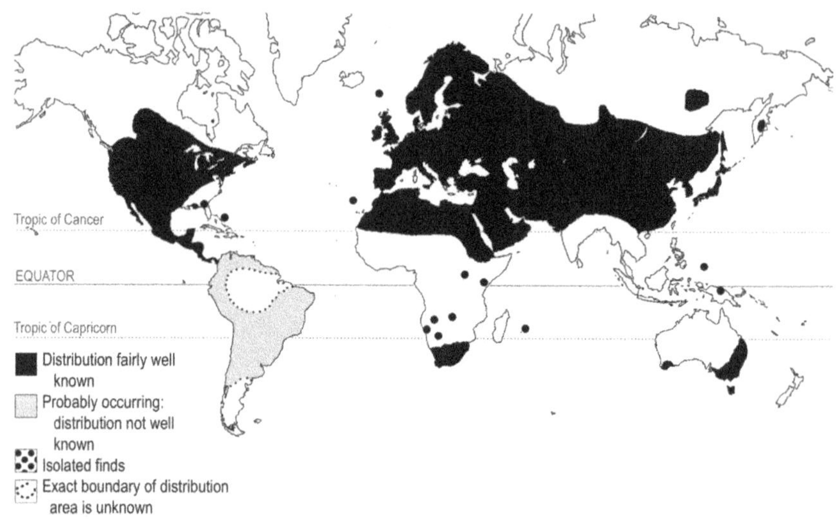


Fig. 10. World-wide distribution of *Phragmites* (van der Toorn, 1972, redrawn).

Reeds spread by seed—the seeds/fruits are blown by the wind, and only a few will land on ground which is damp, not nutrient-poor, not shaded and not liable to deep flooding or severe frosts. What is deep? Up to three-quarters or so of the shoots must be enough above water level, in the air, for the leaves to be able to make sufficient food through photosynthesis. Reed leaves are land, not water, constructed and should not be flooded for long. This is restrictive and normally means seedlings are found on new marshes—typically abandoned ground or suchlike in Britain. So there are few seedlings, and even fewer developing young plants. Hardly *Brilliant*. But in view of the millennia that *Phragmites* can live by their rhizomes, and the way they can grow, it is seldom there is good habitat without *Phragmites*! In Malta, for example, where drying and disturbance have continued unabated for over a century and the climate is summer-dry (typical Mediterranean), it is fascinating that little plants can

16

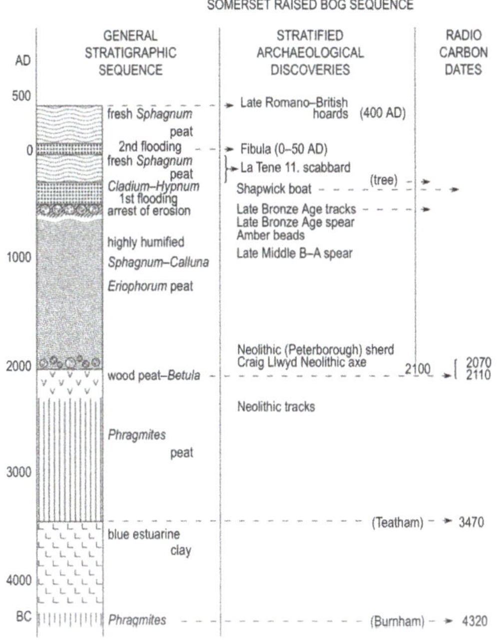



Fig. 11a. Peat section. Somerset Levels, part (after Godwin, 1986). From top to bottom: the most recently formed peat, to the first-formed, oldest. From left to right: dates AD and BC, peat, names of principal peat-forming plants, archaeology, and radiocarbon dates. *Phragmites* is the earliest peat recorded. A sea incursion led to clay deposits before again reedbeds could invade, and this time they stayed for a thousand years. After drying led to birch wood, bog was able to invade (rainwater collecting on surface). Finally, there was a freshwater incursion leading to fen (too few nutrients for reedbed?), followed by bog–fen–bog. Any peat formed after 500 AD has been removed.

11b. Peat section, part, Broadland, Norfolk (after George, 1992 redrawn). The peat on the surface, the newest peat, is at the top, and the peat core goes down as far as possible. Once more, *Phragmites* peat is the lowest soil found (light grey), and it appears four times in the peat core in total over about 1500 years. Any recent peat has been removed. These were two sea incursions (clay), and a drier period between. From left to right: dates, given as BP* before 1950; depth in m; pollen zones (V to VIII, see table right); and substrate zone.

*The abbreviation "BP" has been interpreted retrospectively as "Before Physics"; that refers to the time before nuclear weapons testing artificially altered the proportion of the carbon isotopes in the atmosphere. "Radio Carbon Dating— the initials BP placed after a number means years Before the Present." [*Source*: Wikipedia.org/wiki/Before_Present]

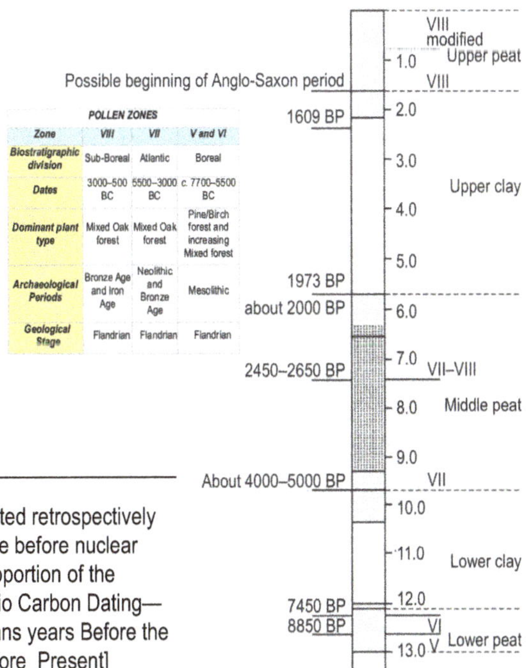

**POLLEN ZONES**

| Zone | VIII | VII | V and VI |
|---|---|---|---|
| Biostratigraphic division | Sub-Boreal | Atlantic | Boreal |
| Dates | 3000–500 BC | 5500–3000 BC | c. 7700–5500 BC |
| Dominant plant type | Mixed Oak forest | Mixed Oak forest | Pine/Birch forest and increasing Mixed forest |
| Archaeological Periods | Bronze Age and Iron Age | Neolithic and Bronze Age | Mesolithic |
| Geological Stage | Flandrian | Flandrian | Flandrian |

remain alive for decades in tiny habitats like cracks in a wall and rock, ready to spread into a wetland should one again become available (Figs 12a–e).

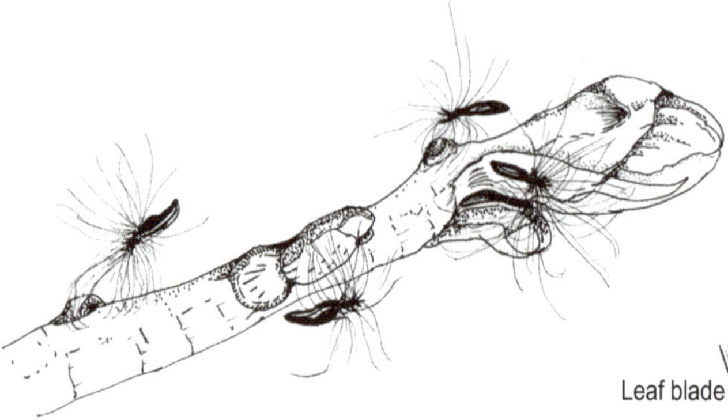

Fig. 12a. Reed fruits clinging by their ring of hairy "pappus" to a sticky tree branch. The ring of hairs can carry the seed for scores of miles.

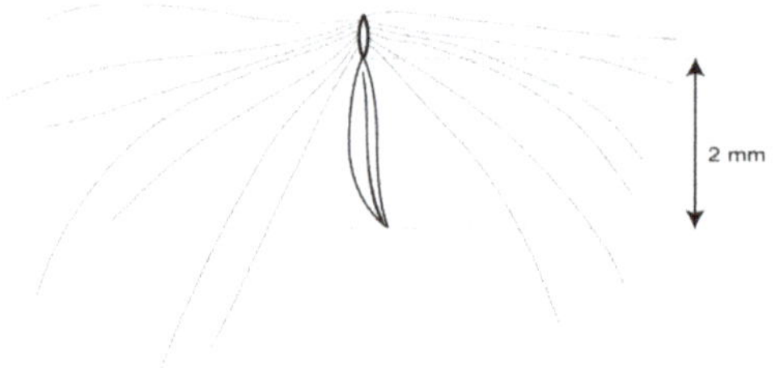

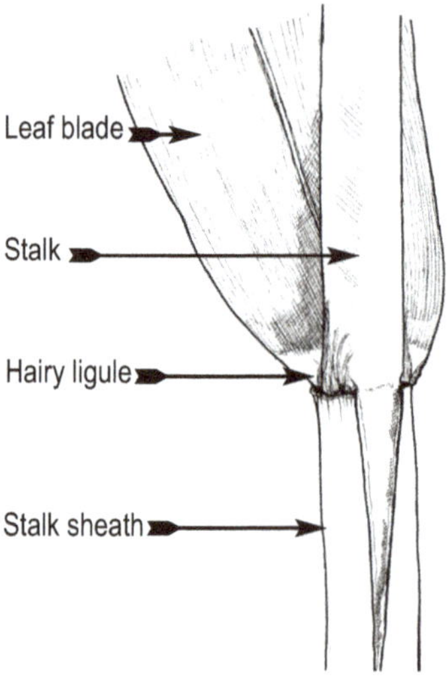

Fig. 12b. Schematic diagram of fruit of *Phragmites australis* (not to scale). This one is probably infertile as it is thin. And parts of a reed (right).

Fig. 12c. Ditch beside salt pans. *Legehalme* continue to cross the ditch in late summer, but are unable to establish on the further side. Nodes may sprout on the *legehalme*, usually into aerial shoots, sometimes into *legehalme*. Where a *legehalme* can establish, the population can advance rapidly.

Fig. 12d. Well-grown *legehalme*, some of its reeds fruiting.

Fig. 12e. (stage i) Seedling growth. Food from the seed supports the plant to the first (or second) stage, which sometimes has a third leaf (stage ii). In unsuitable conditions rapid growth can stop here. The leaf probably turns purplish or brownish, and remains at this stage, years, months, weeks or indeed no significant time. Once the seedling has the food from the habitat to reach the third stage, it can go on to form a proper plant, each shoot being further from, and taller than, the last (stage iii). The final stage shown here has genuine horizontal rhizomes (stage iv). *Live plant resource, Bourn Brook, Cambs.*

And the *legehalme*! Unfortunately these stems have no English name, though they do occur in Britain as on the European Continent and elsewhere. Like so much of *Phragmites* these long (up to 20m or 30m), horizontal stems are governed both genetically (some clones being far more likely to produce them than others) and environmentally (only developing where there is damp soil or open water, little shading and high nutrients). But 20m is quite a long distance, and a plant that can spread 20m a year can colonise empty areas remarkably quickly. There must, however, be a good habitat for the side shoots to grow (Fig. 13)—if dried, flooded, shaded, frozen or eaten, or having inadequate nutrients, they will remain short and probably die in their first winter. If conditions are good, they will probably root and establish in their first summer and be able to grow to 0.5m and more the following summer. Thereafter they will be the same size and density as the reedbed behind. Without *legehalme*, growth of about 1m per year by underground rhizome is common.

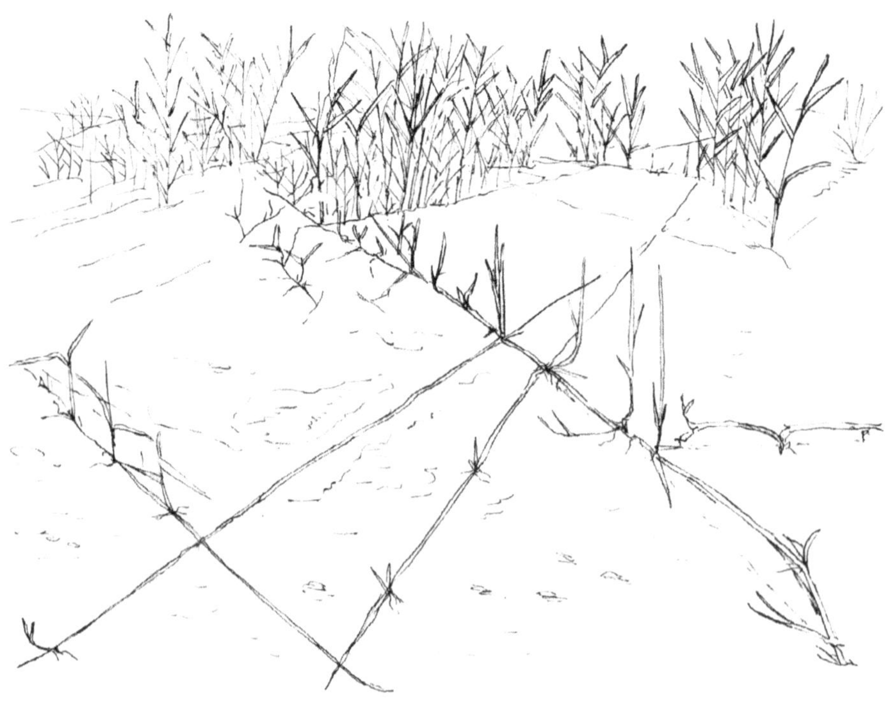

Fig 13. Reed growth showing much lateral growth in obviously the right conditions.

Although reedbeds are usually winter-flooded to 2(+3)m water depth, reeds can grow up to 4+m above water level where, probably, soil is deep and soft, and roots and rhizomes can grow down into the soil until reaching water—or at least dampness. Rhizomes are more cylindrical in dry soil, more flattened in saturated soil (different ecotypes). They have steep-growing basically vertical roots in such soils, except that near the surface, provided the surface is wet—there are tufts of nearer horizontal roots ("water roots") both within the soil and for a few decimetres above it (Fig. 14).

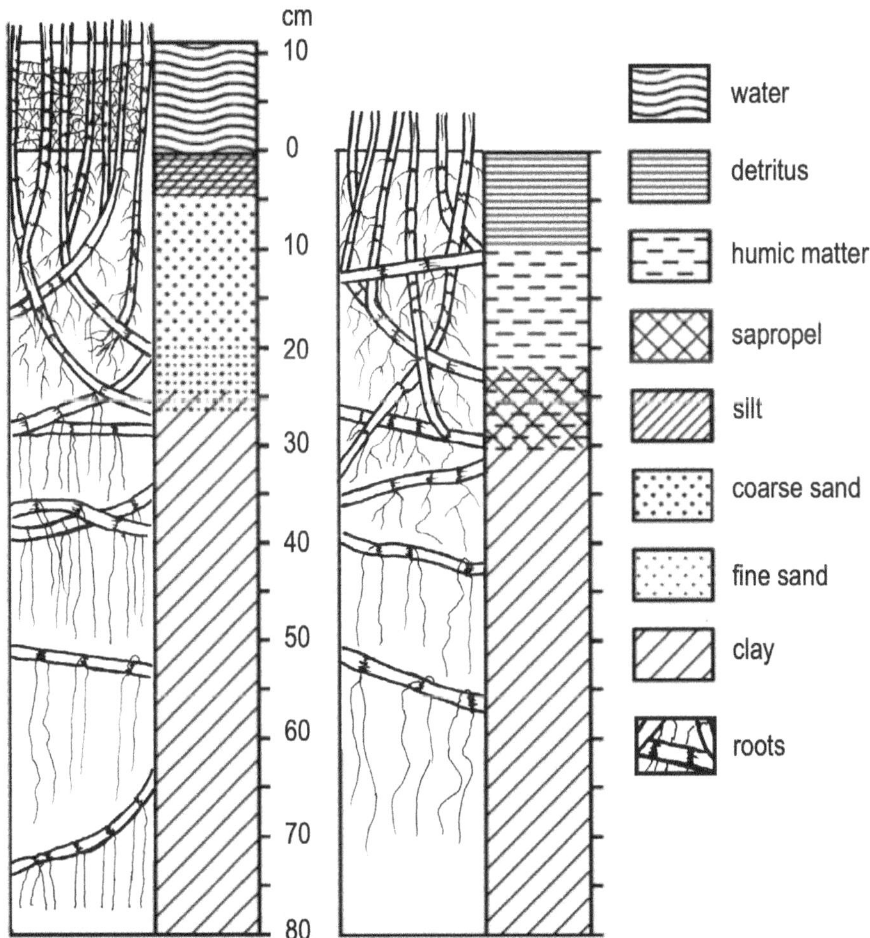


Fig. 14. Variation: genetic and clonal. Rhizomes in two ecotypes in a fish pond in the Czech Republic (after Dykyjová & Hradecká, 1976) left, underwater; right, marshy. The marsh ecotype forms dominant, highly-productive stands, more so than those of the shallow water. They are also wider, with more roots.

The smallest reed—where the tallest shoots in a population barely reach 12cm high—is characteristic of dry edges of reedbeds which are open, trampled, but not over-disturbed. These places are not common and if the habitat is salty—rarer—then the leaves can be very hard—prickly enough to scratch human skin!

In contrast to these small reeds are those growing in woods. Shade depresses growth, and the shoots tend to be under 1.5m tall, may be only 0.5m high and sparse. There is not enough light and the shoots are separated so each can get enough light (*see Fig. 2*), not like open reedbeds where many are crowded together. The leaves here, too, tend to be flat and horizontal to get the best of the light. In the open, there is enough light for the leaves to be oblique.

For nutrients, less research has been done, which may be why there is less peculiarity! Like water regime, there is a wide range of nutrient status in which *Phragmites* grows well. When nutrients are in short supply, in Poor fen, fen-bog or rich-bog, then shoots tend to be sparse and short. Often these habitats are grazed and this is very bad for the reeds. Why? Because the nutrients are in short, or very short, supply and they are eaten! Yes—if a shoot is eaten the nutrients in the shoot are gone. The roots search for the nutrients so readily available in the main reedswamp, but search vainly in grazed areas. When the roots are this affected, developing buds are narrow and few, so shoots are short and sparse. Nutrients being low, leaf blades may be browning or even brown instead of bright green with chlorophyll which is composed of many chemicals.

The same brown is seen in young seedlings, at the 2-leaf stage, which is when they start to need nutrients from the soil, not just from the fruit itself. The seedlings can last at least a couple of years in ordinary (good) soil. With limited resources, research on this point was limited to two years, but it is likely that, with more time and resources, the seedlings may have proved to last at least double this time. Also, when a crystal of phosphate fertiliser was pushed down beside each seedling, it is extraordinary how quickly growth started, the leaves turned green, new leaves appeared, and the young plant grew vigorously.

Less common is the other nutrient-poor habitat, the calcium-dominant one, found near for example, limestone springs. Here in fact there are plenty of nutrients as is shown when the soil dries and reverts to normal. But now in the wet soil, the very high calcium level somehow also blocks the absorption of something—or things—and the reed cannot grow. Like the bog-reed, the

22

shoots come up sparse and short. There is a difference, though. Here the leaf blades grow large (normal size, not small, appropriate to height, like the bog-reeds).

Interested? Not exactly *Brilliant*, but have you, the reader, found as much of interest for any other plant?

## Uses

What value is *Phragmites*? That depends on what is meant by *value*! It may mean monetary worth, or in contrast, that which is worthy of esteem for its own sake, or again the worth in respect of personal qualities, or the liking of something. Well, it will be obvious to the reader that, in this book, reeds rank high in the liking of something! Also, for being worthy of esteem—for the habitat it creates, the acres of reedswamp, the numerous invertebrates, micro-organisms and birds, mammals and so on that it creates habitat for, the peat it creates, and therefore the landscape formed by that peat.

What about monetary worth? Since recorded history—in writing or in peat!—reeds have been used for thatching near the wetlands in which they grow. This is a commercial use. Likewise, if there is need, peat, dry enough to cut out. Both are products which can be bartered or bought. So can grazing, but since reeds grow from the tip, spring grazing though certainly sellable, is not sustainable as it decreases and may ultimately kill the reedbed. Another common use was wall-stuffing.

A small but important use for many centuries was writing—reeds as pen nibs. This is less efficient than papyrus and goose feathers, and of course far less efficient than the steel nib which replaced these, but in the absence of anything better, was possible—and used from at least Ancient Egyptian times. (Remember very few people were literate, so a letter could be assumed to be secret, Gordon 1926.)

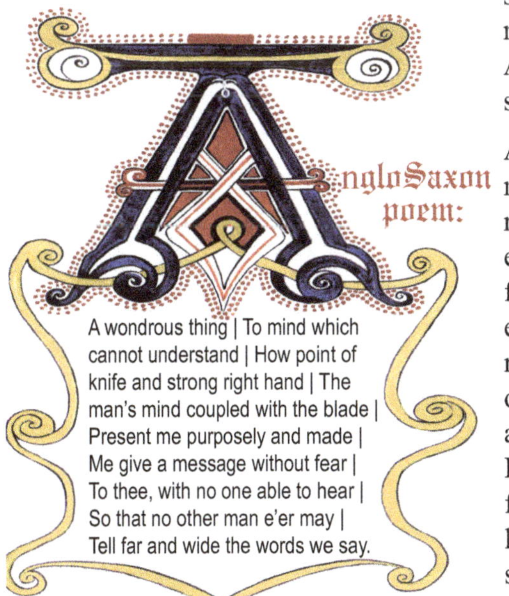

**Following are incidental but widespread and valuable uses of reed:**

- Cleaning water. Reedbeds clean water, filter, transform substances, etc., the water passing through. This useful function has been exploited commercially in the latter part of the twentieth and into the twenty-first centuries, and constructed wetlands for water cleaning have spread countrywide. The disadvantage is that much space is needed—and, with the years, less and less space remains in Great Britain.
- Fish habitat
- Food habitat
- Furniture
- Mats
- Fans
- Hermits and holy places (St Guthlac), as remote, or as being demon-ridden and needing exorcism (malaria?)

**Recorded minor or local uses include:**

art
arrows
baskets
beads
beds
bird nests
buildings (walls—reed or reed-earth), thatch
canoes (bitumen-coated) and other boats
cigarettes
containers
cordage
crafts for tourism
crates
drinks (including alcoholic)
emetic
erosion protection (recent, on banks)
farm litter
ferries
firelighters
fish traps
flute
games
hats
hides
insulation mats
knives
looms
malting
matting
mattresses
ornament
paintbrushes
paper (mostly poor quality)
pillow stuffing
pipe stems (tobacco)
pipes (music)
pipes (transporting water)
raising water level in marshes to allow non-flooded houses to be built
recreation: rambling, camping, photography, nature study, shooting, fishing, boating, swimming, bird watching
reedboard
salad
science: pollen analysis, composition, searching for artefacts, history
sieves
sleeping mats (leaves)
spears
sugar (sucking young reed shoots)
traps
walking sticks

**So, *Boring? Belligerent? Brilliant?***

# Different wetland species and how they interact

Introduction

*Good light* can arise from unusual sources such as:

- animal damage, for example, grazing, walking, pheasants, pests;
- severe late frosts giving open patches in June;
- human impact.

*Damp but unflooded habitats* can come from unlikely sources, for example:

- unusual drought in early summer;
- raised parts, for example, new clods of soil, past peat cutting.

*Competition with* **Carex paniculata** (Greater tussock-sedge, Fig. 15).

*Carex paniculata* is the great tussock sedge, with tussocks reaching over 1m high. As a dominant plant it grows in nutrient-medium, usually calcium-rich places, which are shallow flooded part or all of the year. This means it is a habitat in which *Phragmites* can also dominate. *Carex paniculata* relies on seeds for propagation and without young tussocks the community is not sustainable. The leaves cast heavy shade beside the tussock, but as the tussocks are separate, there is light shade, or even open glades between them. *Phragmites*, of course, being rhizomatous and taller, when able to, forms a complete shading canopy (Fig. 16).

A well-grown, five-month old tussock has 3–5 shoots, 15–30cm high and is therefore able to stand winter flooding of 10–20cm deep. Within dominant *Phragmites*, *Carex*

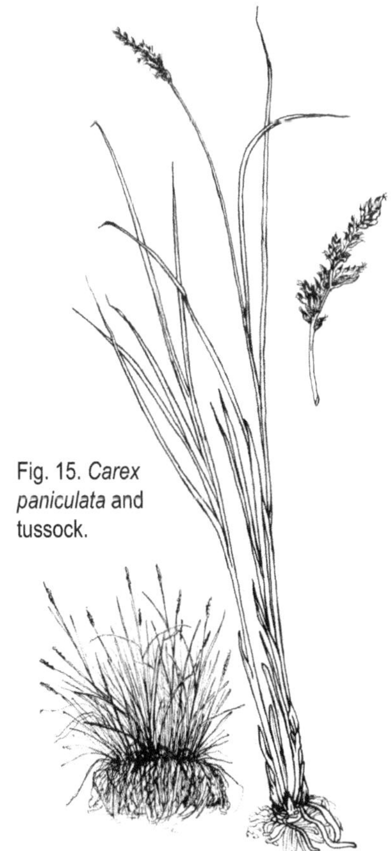

Fig. 15. *Carex paniculata* and tussock.

*paniculata*, once established in a window of opportunity, continues as spindly, weak young tussocks, looking as though shade will kill them by next year. In fact, after 15 years the tussocks can widen and grow up, the tough leaves thrust sideways and push the reeds away and *Carex paniculata* dominates over *Phragmites* (Fig 17). Where *Carex paniculata* is plentiful, it can dominate over *Phragmites*; where it does not dominate, the reedbed remains. Dominant *Carex paniculata* has a restricted nutrient range. It is also not found in deep water or (sustainably) in unflooded areas. So, though locally it can do better, over its whole range *Phragmites* dominates.

*Competition with **Schoenus nigricans*** (Black bog-rush, Fig. 18) is a smaller tussock species, also growing in fens. *Phragmites* towers over it even more than over *Carex paniculata*. So, if dense and tall, *Phragmites* completely

Fig. 16. *Carex paniculata* succeeding *Phragmites* (Yvette Bower, in Haslam, 2003). *Carex paniculata* grows in *Phragmites* shade and when large enough, pushes *Phragmites* away. By the time this tussock dies, other tussocks are present.

Fig. 17. *Carex paniculata* is not rare, but only grows in suitable habitats in water or boggy ground. As each plant grows, the slowly developing tussock-towers form perfect hiding places for vulnerable aquatic species such as water voles (*Arvicola amphibius*). Individual tussocks can grow up to 1.5m across and 1m high.

shades it. Unlike *Carex paniculata, Schoenus nigricans* is not shade-tolerant. The outcome, this time, is surely certain? Well, it is if *Phragmites* is dense and tall, which is only in a disturbed and dried *Schoenus nigricans* community, for in fens it forms the calcium-dominated community par excellence—the one where even nutrient-medium species cannot do well, or grow at all. *Phragmites* is sparse and short, unable to dominate or shade anything, quite apart from its early-yellowing thick leaves and shorter growing season.

Tussocks, in due course, must die, and if not replaced, their community dies, and *Phragmites* again takes over!

These are just a few examples of how competition does or does not work. All these, and more, interact and control the outcome of competition. *Phragmites* of course grows as an associated species in a remarkably wide range of communities, in addition to dominating reedbeds. This means that there are a remarkably wide range  of competitive relations! In each community, each plant and each species "tries" to increase its control over the community. The fact that in stable conditions most vegetation remains stable, shows not that all is quiet and calm, but that the state of tension reached by each species in the combination is a sustainable balance.

Interactions between *Phragmites* and other species may be very complex, as with *Carex paniculata* (*see Figs 16–17*), or very simple, as with *Galium aparine* (Cleavers, Goosegrass, Fig. 19). Few general-isations can be given.

Fig. 18. *Schoenus nigricans* is a lowland perennial sedge which grows as individual tussocks growing 20–70cm tall. Its threadlike leaves bear dark brown ligules (where the flowers grow out from the stem). It favours calcareous fen, especially near springs as well as peaty flushes, marshes, bogs and dune-slacks. Incidence of this plant has declined in lowland sites (recorded 1930), and this loss has continued in some areas where numbers were already low. Its distribution is stable (2020) near the western coasts of Britain and in Ireland.

Underwater, in lake stands, the position is simple. Reed has few potential competitors, and addenda like litter mats and root toxins are little. It is in the marshes and fens that these features may be crucial in determining competitive balance, or its timing. It is also on the land that, apart from wet woodland, *Phragmites* was traditionally absent. Before human impact, reedbeds were succeeded by woodland. Stories like those here would not all have occurred before. Remember this when considering the weapons now used: they were not necessarily evolved for the purpose!

## Reedswamp into open water (historically common)

The depth at which *Phragmites* can grow has been recorded at over 4m, but varies with the nutrient status, the substrate texture, the (lack of) scour, and, quite likely the genotype (its genetic makeup). *Phragmites* cannot establish by seed under water so must grow out from the shore or from rhizome pieces, also probably on the shore.

Fig. 19. *Galium aparine* prefers moist soils and can exist in areas with poor drainage. It is an annual herbaceous plant which has hooks (trichomes) by which it attaches itself to host plants, including *Phragmites*. It sprawls over other plants to a spread of 1.5m with individual stems up to half a metre long. It is the characteristic plant that attaches itself to your clothes when you walk through dense ground-foliage. Geese like to feed on it, hence one of its colloquial names being "Goosegrass".

*Phragmites* will not invade far into substrate where it is difficult for its rhizomes to penetrate (rock, etc.), nor where scour will disturb them. It will invade deeper if nutrients are in good supply. A reedswamp, reed patches, or reed absence may result.

There may be other species present. In good conditions a substantial flora of bottom-living (well-submerged mostly rooted), water-filling or floating plants is likely: water lilies, strap-shaped leaved, finely-divided leaved, and rosette species. *Phragmites*, however, is not hindered by these. It is above water level, so if dense enough, it shades all below. To say "competition" is wrong. *Phragmites* ignores them as much as it does the grains of sand. Landwards, there may be rhizomes in denser swards.

## Seasonal patterns

In order to compete, both parties to the competition must be present. Obvious, but a fact not always remembered. In the Mediterranean climate of Malta, for example, tall monocotyledons (reeds, etc.) and trees are summer-green, in the same way as they are further north. However, most other plants are winter-green and die back, or if annuals, die in summer. It is not surprising that *Phragmites* can grow here into drier habitats than in, say, England. Tall herbs and similar competitors are just not there in the growing season.

## Root toxins and short grass

*Juncus subnodulosus* (Blunt-flowered Rush, Fig. 20) is a mat-forming rush, forming a dense sward 0.5–1m high, with a remarkably dense rhizome network just below ground surface. Rhizomes, of course, bear roots. It is not an historical peat-builder. Most dominant plants in East Anglia were developed by management (by mowing, for example, rushes for strewing) in nutrient-medium, semi-dried fen.

In semi-dried fen *Phragmites* is sparse and short and, as buds grow up through the *Juncus subnodulosus* mat, they narrow, not by just the usual 0–2mm, but by 2–5mm. This means narrow and therefore short shoots which have over-short internodes, as well. These stunted reeds cannot form a shading canopy (rarely reaching 1m tall, whilst the normal reed alongside the *Juncus subnodulosus* community, with 15 rather than the usual 10–11 nodes, can

Fig. 20. *Juncus subnodulosus* is a lowland perennial herb which grows in dense stands in fens, marshes, wet meadows and sometimes in brackish water. It is native to Britain and its distribution has declined both before 1930 and since, mainly due to drainage of its preferred habitat.

grow up to 190cm). Additionally, the emergence of *Phragmites* may be two weeks later than in the other types of reed population alongside, and it also dies two weeks earlier, so giving a month less for food production.

If the *Juncus subnodulosus* rhizome mat is broken, as in clods being dug up, then both these hindering factors nearly vanish. Reeds turn green, grow taller, and live longer.

*Calamagrostis canescens* (Purple small-reed, Fig. 21) is a short grass growing where light comes through *Phragmites* beds. If the bed is flooded and/or *Phragmites* can produce a shading canopy, *Calamagrostis canescens* cannot tolerate that and *Phragmites* dominates. If the bed is neither flooded nor shaded, *Calamagrostis canescens* can keep *Phragmites* buds sparse, and itself dominate. This is an unstable relationship. Water regime is primary, plant factors secondary.

Fig. 21. *Calamagrostis canescens* (Purple small-reed) is a perennial herb which grows in lakeside marshes, fen-meadows, tall-herb fens and carr. It forms extensive stands in species-rich vegetation where conditions are favourable.

The Scramblers

*Calystegia sepium* (False bindweed, Fig. 22) and *Galium aparine* (*see Fig. 19*) are unusual in that they can both bring down reeds to the ground, scrambling over the reeds and pulling them down, so that over large swathes the reeds are flat on the ground by late summer. However, this is only temporary, and the following year it is unlikely that *Phragmites* has weakened, so the balance of dominance is therefore not altered.

Fig. 22. *Calystegia sepium* which can spread over, and flatten, *Phragmites*. The photograph shows *Calystegia sepium* scrambling up low-hanging willow branches in a damp spot on the bank edge of the River Itchen, Hampshire (September 2011).

Management of reedbeds for some (human) use

Commercial (and ex-commercial) reedbeds have been used and managed for centuries (or they can be now). Winter cutting removes young woody plants before they become large, shading, invading trees. It gives bare ground in spring, and this means greater temperature fluctuations which, in turn, means more *Phragmites* buds at emergence and these emerging earlier, so there is a shading canopy of *Phragmites* before its competitors develop.

*Cladium mariscus* (Swamp sawgrass, Great fen-sedge, Fig. 23) is a minor thatching species. It has perennial leaves which store much food. Annual winter cutting of a mixed stand leads to *Phragmites* dominance (bad for sedge). Conversely, summer cutting every 3–4 years leads to *Cladium mariscus* dominance. So dominance is generally due to the type of management. In order for *Phragmites* to develop and dominate, nutrients must be added from outside.

Poor fen (*Parvocaricetum*) has more nutrients than bog but, unlike bog, is often caused by and due to management—past and present. Light grazing is or was common and this, with the sub-adequate nutrients, mean that it is difficult for *Phragmites* to be more than a short, sparse associate. If (as happened in Wicken Fen, Cambridgeshire) nutrients are increased, then *Phragmites* can grow taller and become more frequent. Without management, this could lead to a reedbed in the course of time—or, of course, to carr and woodland.

Fig. 23. *Cladium mariscus* is native to Britain. It is a lowland rhizomatous perennial preferring a low–moderate nutrient regime, usually growing on peat. It is also found in swamps, along lake and pond margins and streams, as well as in tall-herb fens and in open fen carr (wet or damp woodland). It can grow up to 2.5m in height, in dense clumps. Foliage turns yellow-gold in autumn. It used to be an important material for thatching roofs. Incidence has declined recently due to drainage, eutrophication (raised nutrient levels) and scrub invasion of its habitat.

Tall Herb fens are found in dried, ex-managed fens and marshes, and most of the species are from 1m to over 1.5m high, much the same as the *Phragmites* living sparsely within the fen (or locally, by dykes, or indeed not at all). This community can be stable over decades, but it is not viable. Although the dry soil and generally numerous invertebrates militate against tree invasion, it happens (as for sallow) unless management changes.

## Ways to Dominate

There are many ways in which one species can dominate another, but the principal **weapons** of *Phragmites* (and its competitors) are as follows.

Plant factors

**Shading** (conversely, preventing a potentially shading plant from growing tall).

**Litter mat preventing new growth** (and ability to withstand the litter mat of other species).

**Production of toxins** (from the roots) which will hinder good growth of other species. (Conversely, tolerance to such toxins from other species.)

Development of thick, tall **advancing margins** which pass through other vegetation like a tank, and ability to re-grow in the less vigorous growth behind the advancing margin (Fig. 24).

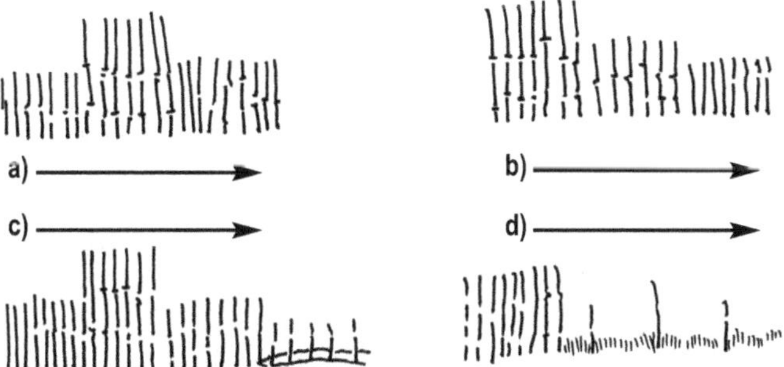


Fig. 24. *Phragmites* Clones with advancing margin, vertical plan (diagrammatic), Rosyth, Scotland (Haslam, 2003, redrawn). Arrows indicate direction of growth. a) A single ring this year. Last year's shoots are the tallest here, but other height patterns occur. b) and c) show a second and shorter ring of shoots, grown in late summer. In b) this second ring is from new rhizomes, in c) it is from *legehalme* shoots, usually shorter and sparser. d) Shoots of this year and last year are restricted by root competition with the other species, and are very sparse.

**Occupy the space** completely, and do so early in the year before other species can shade it.

**Pull down (so shade) other species** (lodging) and not be pulled down.

All factors **hindering bud development**. To grow well *Phragmites* must grow many buds from the rhizomes, and all factors, plant or otherwise, which restrict this development, also favour the competition.

Have **plant vigour**. (No one knows what this is but *everyone* can recognise it.)

Outside factors acting in mixed stands

**Water level.** Raising water level removes reed and other species not adapted to the new depth. Lowering water level acts in reverse.

**Nutrients.** Nutrient status also determines which species can potentially flourish, grow adequately, or pine and die. Often species of higher nutrient status are more able to shade and suppress others.

**Man's Impact.** This has many effects, primarily to destroy reedbeds by drying and disturbance. Winter harvesting favours reeds, heavy grazing removes it.

**Disease** affecting one species but not another.

**Aeration**. Some species do better where aeration (dryness or moving water) is good.

**Weather**. Lack of sunshine and unexpected lack of water in the growing season lead to shorter shoots, perhaps by half a metre or more. Competitors only a little shorter than *Phragmites* then have an advantage.

**Early growth** can be crucial in determining which species shades.

In **Bogs**, *Phragmites* is larger and more vigorous than the other species so can easily shade them out—where nutrients are high enough for it to occur.

Bog is the other traditional successor of *Phragmites*. Reedbeds form peat (Fig. 25a–g).

*Sphagnum* (bog moss) can invade:

- when its propagules can reach the site;
- when rainwater can accumulate on the ground surface;
- where nutrient-richer flooding is absent or very rare;
- where the soil is bare beneath the reeds (no thick litter mat).

Fig. 25a. *Sphagnum* Reedland. *Sphagnum* on fen surface can hold many times its weight in water. Once it is established on a surface, the water is held, just below the moss tips covering the surface. Rainwater lenses occur (convex-shaped layer of fresh groundwater). Evapotranspiration is reduced because the main water is sub-surface. Downwards loss is reduced because the substrate below (peat, rock, etc.) is hardly pervious. Sideways loss is reduced because of the low slope and texture of the vegetation and peat. Where the conditions are met, the surface water is acid and nutrient deficient, and bog grows. (There are at least two *Phragmites* clones here.)

When the reedbed is flooded regularly or constantly the nutrient-rich water of the reedbed floods any *Sphagnum* and prevents its growth. *Sphagnum* invades only where there are rainwater pools. The soil is nutrient-rich, but the rainwater is not, and *Sphagnum* can grow. Its leaves and tips absorb water, and hold it in, so water accumulates within and between the shoots which is difficult to dry out. Gradually, *Sphagnum* spreads, becomes thicker, and more bog-like species arrive to join, and supersede the fen species.

Holt Country Park, Norfolk (October 2020) has a varied landscape pattern, including mixed woodland, heather and gorse scrubland (Fig. 25b) woodland scrub (silver birch, alder, willow, Fig. 25c), marsh (mosses and rushes, Fig. 25d), and boggy marsh (Fig. 25e–f). *Phragmites* are sparse here because conditions favour *Sphagnum* (Fig. 25g).

Fig. 25b. Heather and gorse grow on the chalky heath slopes which lead down to rainwater pools in the valley.

Fig. 25c. In damp areas, *Sphagnum* is growing quite well, interlaced with saplings of silver birch, alder and willow.

Fig. 25d. Further down the slope, *Sphagnum* is interlaced with marsh grasses and rushes in the damp, nutrient-rich soil.

Fig. 25e. At the bottom of the slope is a large rain-water pool. "Spongy" Sphagnum is growing well towards the water's edge.

*Sphagnum* and *Phragmites* can co-exist for a relatively long period. The *Phragmites* rhizomes are well down in the mineral-rich peat. The *Sphagnum* has its own nutrient-deficient rainwater. Both grow. The *Phragmites* is no longer forming peat but, if conditions stay stable, *Sphagnum* in contrast builds peat with its tips constantly growing upwards and spreading, and its old stems and leaves turning into peat. It stays wet because the top absorbs rainwater, and the rest keeps it. *Sphagnum* peat therefore grows upwards and, to keep pace, the *Phragmites* rhizomes and bud position grow upwards too, basing growth, as usual, on the ground surface which here is the top of the *Sphagnum*. Therefore gradually first the upper part then all of the *Phragmites* plant comes to be within *Sphagnum* peat, and the plant dies from nutrient deficiency. Unless there is human impact, the bogs will grow.

Fig. 25f. Around the edges of the trampled (ponies) rain-water pool, *Sphagnum* has a thick litter mat beneath its colourful growing tips.

Fig. 25g. There were a few shoots of *Phragmites* (red circles) on the drier side of the rain-water pool. But these were very sparse and small.

Competition is indirect. *Phragmites* could perfectly well shade out *Sphagnum*, especially if aided by a thick litter mat. If it does so, there is no *Sphagnum*. Similarly, if there is drying (as too often in England), there are neither rain-water pools for bog peat, nor river-flooding for fen.

## Reedswamp to Trees

Tree invaders of *Phragmites* beds are usually *Salix* (sallows and willows), or *Alnus glutinosa* (alder). Sallow carr is very common. It tolerates stagnant habitats, but not calcium-dominant fens (where it is replaced by *Betula*, birch). Sallow only invades when the bed is unflooded for part of the year for a few years whilst the tree seeds first germinate, then start to grow and become established. To develop from reed to sallow-carr with sparse *Phragmites* in the undergrowth can take between a few decades to a century or more. Sallow seed production is profuse in spring, as is its germination in early summer. Young plants abound wherever they can grow and can flourish in good light, damp but not flooded land—preferably without the numerous invertebrates found in a Tall Herb habitat.

Invasion therefore depends on "accident"—the "window of opportunity" that allows sallow seeds to arrive where they can germinate, become established, and not be drowned or eaten until the saplings are large enough to withstand flooding and be only partly eaten. Sallow saplings may start in the open, but frequently the reedbed closes round them and they are shaded. Sallow then grows very slowly, but does find enough light filtering through the canopy to stay alive. As the years pass and the saplings look constantly unhealthy, even on the point of death, they grow taller. Finally, sallow being taller than reed, the bushes emerge above the reed canopy. Now suddenly they can use the light and grow and spread fast. A reedbed hiding small, sparse saplings rapidly becomes carr, the shaded reed declining into short, sparse, frail shoots. Even if alder invades the sallow as it dries further, the reed will remain much the same—unless and until wet woodland becomes dry woodland.

Windows of opportunity may happen this year, or not for 25 years and then only for a few sallows. Predictions are impossible except that if the fen is dried and unflooded and Tall Herb takes over, invasion seems to be much slower (seeds eaten by invertebrates? Too dry?) and if the fen is then turned to grass or arable, the window will not happen at all!

## Conclusion

People visit reedbeds for leisurely walks, research, harvesting or main-tenance—if walking or working alone, they may feel almost a magic, refreshing, renewing atmosphere and, for a researcher, perhaps an intensifying wish to learn. In deplorable "science-speak", this is known as the "spiritual-societal effect".

**Solitary? Peaceful? Other-worldly? Only for people!**

**For the reed it is an intense but silent battle for survival.**

There is no peace in the reedbed for *Phragmites*. There is a struggle for existence. There may or may not be a struggle by the plant for the existence of the reedbed, or that may be done for example by the water regime alone. There is certainly a struggle between the shoots on a single plant, small shoots frequently succumbing to food competition from large ones.

In Europe, the struggle for community existence in the hazy band "twixt land and water", is usually won by *Phragmites*. In the Americas, Australasia, Africa and much of Asia, it is usually won by other reedswamp species. Even in Europe there is more than just the wide reedswamp. There is the isolated clump, the hectares of Poor fen, the fringes around dykes and drains, the patches in bogs and green fields and, in particular, the willow-reed bands (*Salix-Phragmites*) enclosing streams which have not been drained, both in flatter lowland and on gentle slopes up in fertile wooded mountains. These bands have dominant reed, but often 1–1.5m high, not the taller reedbed of the lakes, or the giant reedbeds of lakes in some warm-summer, more eastern area like Turkey, Iraq, North Africa or the Danube Delta.

In England we still have wonderful places like the Norfolk Broads with nature reserves such as Strumpshaw Fen situated on the River Yare in Norfolk, about six miles east of Norwich. It is a RSPB Nature Reserve and the reserve itself has a full range of broadland habitats, flora and fauna, including many stands of *Phragmites*, otters, bitterns, marsh harriers, as well as its resident and visiting warblers (Fig. 26) and the fabulous Norfolk Swallowtail butterfly (Fig. 27). (…And, in south-west Britain, the wonderful Somerset Levels. *See "STREAM STORY I: A Riveting Riverscape—River Brue, Somerset"* in this Series.)…

…And also Fen Drayton Lakes RSPB Nature Reserve in Cambridgeshire which began life as a flooded sand and gravel quarry next to riverside meadows. Now a huge variety of wildlife has been drawn to the area, including otters, dragonflies, ducks, swans and geese. There is something to see (and hear) all year round (Fig. 28).

Fig. 28. The title of this little book, "REED—ON THE EDGE", is typified in this photograph, taken at RSPB Fen Drayton Lakes Nature Reserve (Cambridgeshire) in December 2011. Note the small band of old *Phragmites* along the lake edge and the willow tree behind. Across the lake is a much larger stand of reed—also **"On the Edge"**!

# REFERENCES

*Beowulf.* Anon. Anglo Saxon (Old English) Epic Poem written anonymously around 975 AD, now called *The Nowell Codex* is housed in the British Library. (Poem first printed by Thorkelin in 1815). View old and modern versions of this poem on our River Friend Website: **[http://riverfriend.tinasfineart.uk/resources/]**

British Library. *Life of Guthlac* (the "Guthlac Roll" or "*Vita Sancti Guthlaci*"). Vellum Roll created 1175–1215. The Benedictine Abbey of Crowland, Lincolnshire. Harley Roll Y 6.

Colgrave, B. (1956) *Felix's Life of Saint Guthlac.* Edited with translation, introduction and notes by Bertram Colgrave. Pp. xv + 205. Cambridge: University Press.

Ditlhogo M.K.M., James R., Laurence B.R. & Sutherland W.J. (1992) The effects of conservation management of reed beds. I. The invertebrates. *Journal of Applied Ecology*, **29**, 265-276

Dykyjová D & Hradecká D. 1976. Production ecology of *Phragmites communis*, 1. Relations of two ecotypes to the microclimate and nutrient conditions of habitat. *Folia Geobotanica Phytotaxonomica*, Praha, **11**: 23–61.

George M. 1992. *The land use, ecology and conservation of Broadland.* Chichester: Packard Press.

Godwin H. 1981 and 1986. *History of the British Flora.* Cambridge: University Press.

Gordon, R.K., transl. (1926) *Anglo-Saxon Poetry*, Dent & Sons Ltd, London, UK.

Haslam, S.M. (2003). *Understanding Wetlands: Fen, Bog And Marsh.* Taylor & Francis, London, 296 pp. ISBN 0-415-25704-8. Original cartoon drawn by Y. Bower.

Haslam, S.M. (2010) *A Book of Reed (Phragmites australis* (Cav.) Trin. ex Steudel, *Phragmites communis* Trin.). Forrest Text, Cardigan.

Paris Matthew. (1250). *Historia Anglorum (A History of England).* British Library. b. c. 1200, d. 1259. English Benedictine monk and chronicler of the *St Alban's Chronicles.* Also illustrated *The Life of St Alban.*

Toorn J van der. 1972. Variability of *Phragmites australis* [Cav.] Trin. ex Steudel in relation to the environment. *Van Zee Tot Land*, **48**. 's-Gravenhage.

# THE RIVER FRIEND SERIES

This series of small books is designed for people with a general or specific interest in rivers.
Please visit the River Friend Website for an up to-date list of
PUBLISHED Titles: **http://www.riverfriend.tinasfineart.uk**

**Standalone* Titles in the Series include:**

*A PROLOGUE TO THE SERIES: Plant identification and Glossary of Terms* (ISBN 978 1 9162096 2 6)
*DRYING UP* (ISBN 978 1 9162096 1 9)
*STREAM STORY I: A Riveting Riverscape—River Brue, Somerset*
(ISBN 978 1 9162096 0 2)
*INTERPRET: What do Plants Tell us?* (ISBN 978 1 9162096 5 7)
*Vegetation Changes Over Time. Is there FREEZE FRAME?*
(ISBN 978 1 9162096 6 4)
*REED—ON THE EDGE* **(ISBN 978 1 9162096 4 0)**
*An Introduction to the WATER FRAMEWORK DIRECTIVE*
(ISBN 978 1 9162096 3 3)
*WATER: Clean and Dirty* (ISBN 978 1 9162096 7 1)
*STREAM STORY II: A Brook in Transit: Bourn Brook, Cambs*
(ISBN 978 1 9162096 8 8)
*CHANGE: What a Disaster!* (ISBN 978 1 9162096 9 5)
*LOOK AT THE BOTTOM*
*How to lose Fresh Water in Under Two Centuries. The Example of MALTA*
*VEGETATION PATTERNS*
*IN THE WATER*
*THE WATERS OF WELLS*
*RESTORE, REHABILITATE, IMPROVE*
*AWFUL ALIENS*
*WHAT RIVERS DO FOR US*

*Each book is about a different subject so the series can be read in any order

## About the Authors

**Sylvia Haslam** is a botanist and river culture, etc., specialist. Anyone wanting to find out more should look at the publications list on her website (http://www.riversandreeds.co.uk). Her publications specific to this series are listed in the book entitled *A PROLOGUE TO THE SERIES: Plant identification and Glossary of Terms.*

**Tina Bone** has worked as a self-employed Desktop Publisher for many years until she changed career to work as a Professional Artist from March 2005. To view Tina's resumé and artwork please visit her website: http://www.tinasfineart.uk.